Studies and Essays:
Censorship and Art

John Galsworthy

ESSAYS ON CENSORSHIP AND ART

By John Galsworthy

"Je vous dirai que l'exces est toujours un mal. "

—ANATOLE FRANCE

CONTENTS:

ABOUT CENSORSHIP

Since, time and again, it has been proved, in this country of free institutions, that the great majority of our fellow-countrymen consider the only Censorship that now obtains amongst us, namely the Censorship of Plays, a bulwark for the preservation of their comfort and sensibility against the spiritual researches and speculations of bolder and too active spirits—it has become time to consider whether we should not seriously extend a principle, so grateful to the majority, to all our institutions.

For no one can deny that in practice the Censorship of Drama works with a smooth swiftness—a lack of delay and friction unexampled in any public office. No troublesome publicity and tedious postponement for the purpose of appeal mar its efficiency. It is neither hampered by the Law nor by the slow process of popular election. Welcomed by the overwhelming majority of the public; objected to only by such persons as suffer from it, and a negligible faction, who, wedded pedantically to liberty of the subject, are resentful of summary powers vested in a single person responsible only to his own 'conscience'—it is amazingly, triumphantly, successful.

Why, then, in a democratic State, is so valuable a protector of the will, the interests, and pleasure of the majority not bestowed on other branches of the public being? Opponents of the Censorship of Plays have been led by the absence of such other Censorships to conclude

1

that this Office is an archaic survival, persisting into times that have outgrown it. They have been known to allege that the reason of its survival is simply the fact that Dramatic Authors, whose reputation and means of livelihood it threatens, have ever been few in number and poorly organised—that the reason, in short, is the helplessness and weakness of the interests concerned. We must all combat with force such an aspersion on our Legislature. Can it even for a second be supposed that a State which gives trial by Jury to the meanest, poorest, most helpless of its citizens, and concedes to the greatest criminals the right of appeal, could have debarred a body of reputable men from the ordinary rights of citizenship for so cynical a reason as that their numbers were small, their interests unjoined, their protests feeble? Such a supposition were intolerable! We do not in this country deprive a class of citizens of their ordinary rights, we do not place their produce under the irresponsible control of one not amenable to Law, by any sort of political accident! That would indeed be to laugh at Justice in this Kingdom! That would indeed be cynical and unsound! We must never admit that there is no basic Justice controlling the edifice of our Civic Rights. We do, we must, conclude that a just and well-considered principle underlies this despotic Institution; for surely, else, it would not be suffered to survive for a single moment! Pom! Pom!

If, then, the Censorship of Plays be just, beneficent, and based on a well-considered principle, we must rightly inquire what good and logical reason there is for the absence of Censorship in other departments of the national life. If Censorship of the Drama be in the real interests of the people, or at all events in what the Censor for the time being conceives to be their interest—then Censorships of Art, Literature, Religion, Science, and Politics are in the interests of the people, unless it can be proved that there exists essential difference between the Drama and these other branches of the public being. Let us consider whether there is any such essential difference.

It is fact, beyond dispute, that every year numbers of books appear which strain the average reader's intelligence and sensibilities to an unendurable extent; books whose speculations are totally unsuited to normal thinking powers; books which contain views of morality divergent from the customary, and discussions of themes unsuited to the young person; books which, in fine, provide the greater Public with no pleasure whatsoever, and, either by harrowing their feelings or offending their good taste, cause them real pain.

It is true that, precisely as in the case of Plays, the Public are protected by a vigilant and critical Press from works of this description; that, further, they are protected by the commercial instinct of the Libraries, who will not stock an article which may offend their customers—just as, in the case of Plays, the Public are protected by the common-sense of theatrical Managers; that, finally, they are protected by the Police and the Common Law of the land. But despite all these protections, it is no uncommon thing for an average citizen to purchase one of these disturbing or dubious books. Has he, on discovering its true nature, the right to call on the bookseller to refund its value? He has not. And thus he runs a danger obviated in the case of the Drama which has the protection of a prudential Censorship. For this reason alone, how much better, then, that there should exist a paternal authority (some, no doubt, will call it grand-maternal—but sneers must not be confounded with argument) to suppress these books before appearance, and safeguard us from the danger of buying and possibly reading undesirable or painful literature!

A specious reason, however, is advanced for exempting Literature from the Censorship accorded to Plays. He—it is said—who attends the performance of a play, attends it in public, where his feelings may be harrowed and his taste offended, cheek by jowl with boys, or women of all ages; it may even chance that he has taken to this entertainment his wife, or the young persons of his household. He—on the other hand—who reads a book, reads it in privacy. True; but the wielder of this argument has clasped his fingers round a two-edged blade. The very fact that the book has no mixed audience removes from Literature an element which is ever the greatest check on licentiousness in Drama. No manager of a theatre, —a man of the world engaged in the acquisition of his livelihood, unless guaranteed by the license of the Censor, dare risk the presentment before a mixed audience of that which might cause an 'emeute' among his clients. It has, indeed, always been observed that the theatrical manager, almost without exception, thoughtfully recoils from the responsibility that would be thrust on him by the abolition of the Censorship. The fear of the mixed audience is ever suspended above his head. No such fear threatens the publisher, who displays his wares to one man at a time. And for this very reason of the mixed audience; perpetually and perversely cited to the contrary by such as have no firm grasp of this matter, there is a greater necessity for a Censorship on Literature than for one on Plays.

Further, if there were but a Censorship of Literature, no matter how dubious the books that were allowed to pass, the conscience of no reader need ever be troubled. For, that the perfect rest of the public conscience is the first result of Censorship, is proved to certainty by the protected Drama, since many dubious plays are yearly put before the play-going Public without tending in any way to disturb a complacency engendered by the security from harm guaranteed by this beneficent, if despotic, Institution. Pundits who, to the discomfort of the populace, foster this exemption of Literature from discipline, cling to the old-fashioned notion that ulcers should be encouraged to discharge themselves upon the surface, instead of being quietly and decently driven into the system and allowed to fester there.

The remaining plea for exempting Literature from Censorship, put forward by unreflecting persons: That it would require too many Censors—besides being unworthy, is, on the face of it, erroneous. Special tests have never been thought necessary in appointing Examiners of Plays. They would, indeed, not only be unnecessary, but positively dangerous, seeing that the essential function of Censorship is protection of the ordinary prejudices and forms of thought. There would, then, be no difficulty in securing tomorrow as many Censors of Literature as might be necessary (say twenty or thirty); since all that would be required of each one of them would be that he should secretly exercise, in his uncontrolled discretion, his individual taste. In a word, this Free Literature of ours protects advancing thought and speculation; and those who believe in civic freedom subject only to Common Law, and espouse the cause of free literature, are championing a system which is essentially undemocratic, essentially inimical to the will of the majority, who have certainly no desire for any such things as advancing thought and speculation. Such persons, indeed, merely hold the faith that the People, as a whole, unprotected by the despotic judgments of single persons, have enough strength and wisdom to know what is and what is not harmful to themselves. They put their trust in a Public Press and a Common Law, which deriving from the Conscience of the Country, is openly administered and within the reach of all. How absurd, how inadequate this all is we see from the existence of the Censorship on Drama.

Having observed that there is no reason whatever for the exemption of Literature, let us now turn to the case of Art. Every picture hung in a gallery, every statue placed on a pedestal, is exposed to the public stare of a mixed company. Why, then, have we no Censorship to protect us from the possibility of encountering works that bring blushes to the cheek of the young person? The reason cannot be that the proprietors of Galleries are more worthy of trust than the managers of Theatres; this would be to make an odious distinction which those very Managers who uphold the Censorship of Plays would be the first to resent. It is true that Societies of artists and the proprietors of Galleries are subject to the prosecution of the Law if they offend against the ordinary standards of public decency; but precisely the same liability attaches to theatrical managers and proprietors of Theatres, in whose case it has been found necessary and beneficial to add the Censorship. And in this connection let it once more be noted how much more easily the ordinary standards of public decency can be assessed by a single person responsible to no one, than by the clumsy (if more open) process of public protest. What, then, in the light of the proved justice and efficiency of the Censorship of Drama, is the reason for the absence of the Censorship of Art? The more closely the matter is regarded, the more plain it is, that there is none! At any moment we may have to look upon some painting, or contemplate some statue, as tragic, heart-rending, and dubiously delicate in theme as that censured play "The Cenci, " by one Shelley; as dangerous to prejudice, and suggestive of new thought as the censured "Ghosts, " by one Ibsen. Let us protest against this peril suspended over our heads, and demand the immediate appointment of a single person not selected for any pretentiously artistic feelings, but endowed with summary powers of prohibiting the exhibition, in public galleries or places, of such works as he shall deem, in his uncontrolled discretion, unsuited to average intelligence or sensibility. Let us demand it in the interest, not only of the young person, but of those whole sections of the community which cannot be expected to take an interest in Art, and to whom the purpose, speculations, and achievements of great artists, working not only for to-day but for to-morrow, must naturally be dark riddles. Let us even require that this official should be empowered to order the destruction of the works which he has deemed unsuited to average intelligence and sensibility, lest their creators should, by private sale, make a profit out of them, such as, in the nature of the case, Dramatic Authors are debarred from making out of plays which, having been censured, cannot be played for money. Let us ask this with confidence; for it is not compatible with common justice that there should be any favouring of Painter over Playwright. They are both artists—let them both be measured by the same last!

But let us now consider the case of Science. It will not, indeed cannot, be contended that the investigations of scientific men, whether committed to writing or to speech, are always suited to the taste and capacities of our general public. There was, for example, the well-known doctrine of Evolution, the teachings of Charles Darwin and Alfred Russet Wallace, who gathered up certain facts, hitherto but vaguely known, into presentments, irreverent and startling, which, at the time, profoundly disturbed every normal mind. Not only did religion, as then accepted, suffer in this cataclysm, but our taste and feeling were inexpressibly shocked by the discovery, so emphasised by Thomas Henry Huxley, of Man's descent from Apes. It was felt, and is felt by many to this day, that the advancement of that theory grossly and dangerously violated every canon of decency. What pain, then, might have been averted, what far-reaching consequences and incalculable subversion of primitive faiths checked, if some judicious Censor of scientific thought had existed in those days to demand, in accordance with his private estimate of the will and temper of the majority, the suppression of the doctrine of Evolution.

Innumerable investigations of scientists on subjects such as the date of the world's creation, have from time to time been summarised and inconsiderately sprung on a Public shocked and startled by the revelation that facts which they were accustomed to revere were conspicuously at fault. So, too, in the range of medicine, it would be difficult to cite any radical discovery (such as the preventive power of vaccination), whose unchecked publication has not violated the prejudices and disturbed the immediate comfort of the common mind. Had these discoveries been judiciously suppressed, or pared away to suit what a Censorship conceived to be the popular palate of the time, all this disturbance and discomfort might have been avoided.

It will doubtless be contended (for there are no such violent opponents of Censorship as those who are threatened with the same) that to compare a momentous disclosure, such as the doctrine of Evolution, to a mere drama, were unprofitable. The answer to this ungenerous contention is fortunately plain. Had a judicious Censorship existed over our scientific matters, such as for two hundred years has existed over our Drama, scientific discoveries would have been no more disturbing and momentous than those which we are accustomed to see made on our nicely pruned and tutored stage. For not only would the more dangerous and penetrating scientific truths have been carefully destroyed at birth, but scientists, aware that the results of investigations offensive to accepted notions would be suppressed, would long have ceased to waste their time in search of a knowledge repugnant to average intelligence, and thus foredoomed, and have occupied themselves with services more agreeable to the public taste, such as the rediscovery of truths already known and published.

Indissolubly connected with the desirability of a Censorship of Science, is the need for Religious Censorship. For in this, assuredly not the least important department of the nation's life, we are witnessing week by week and year by year, what in the light of the security guaranteed by the Censorship of Drama, we are justified in terming an alarming spectacle. Thousands of men are licensed to proclaim from their pulpits, Sunday after Sunday, their individual beliefs, quite regardless of the settled convictions of the masses of their congregations. It is true, indeed, that the vast majority of sermons (like the vast majority of plays) are, and will always be, harmonious with the feelings—of the average citizen; for neither priest nor playwright have customarily any such peculiar gift of spiritual daring as might render them unsafe mentors of their fellows; and there is not wanting the deterrent of common-sense to keep them in bounds. Yet it can hardly be denied that there spring up at times men—like John Wesley or General Booth—of such incurable temperament as to be capable of abusing their freedom by the promulgation of doctrine or procedure, divergent from the current traditions of religion. Nor must it be forgotten that sermons, like plays, are addressed to a mixed audience of families, and that the spiritual teachings of a lifetime may be destroyed by ten minutes of uncensored pronouncement from a pulpit, the while parents are sitting, not, as in a theatre vested with the right of protest, but dumb and excoriated to the soul, watching their children, perhaps of tender age, eagerly drinking in words at variance with that which they themselves have been at such pains to instil.

If a set of Censors—for it would, as in the case of Literature, indubitably require more than one (perhaps one hundred and eighty, but, for reasons already given, there should be no difficulty whatever in procuring them) endowed with the swift powers conferred by freedom from the dull tedium of responsibility, and not remarkable for religious temperament, were appointed, to whom all sermons and public addresses on religious subjects must be submitted before delivery, and whose duty after perusal should be to excise all portions not conformable to their private ideas of what was at the moment suitable to the Public's ears, we should be far on the road toward that proper preservation of the status quo so desirable if the faiths and ethical standards of the less exuberantly spiritual masses are to be maintained in their full bloom. As things now stand, the nation has absolutely nothing to safeguard it against religious progress.

We have seen, then, that Censorship is at least as necessary over Literature, Art, Science, and Religion as it is over our Drama. We have now to call attention to the crowning need—the want of a Censorship in Politics.

If Censorship be based on justice, if it be proved to serve the Public and to be successful in its lonely vigil over Drama, it should, and logically must be, extended to all parallel cases; it cannot, it dare not, stop short at— Politics. For, precisely in this supreme branch of the public life are we most menaced by the rule and license of the leading spirit. To appreciate this fact, we need only examine the Constitution of the House of Commons. Six hundred and seventy persons chosen from a population numbering four and forty millions, must necessarily, whatever their individual defects, be citizens of more than average enterprise, resource, and resolution. They are elected for a period that may last five years. Many of them are ambitious; some uncompromising; not a few enthusiastically eager to do something for their country; filled with designs and aspirations for national or social betterment, with which the masses, sunk in the immediate pursuits of life, can in the nature of things have little sympathy. And yet we find these men licensed to pour forth at pleasure, before mixed audiences, checked only by Common Law and Common Sense political utterances which may have the gravest, the most terrific consequences; utterances which may at any moment let loose revolution, or plunge the country into war; which often, as a fact, excite an utter detestation, terror, and mistrust; or shock the most sacred domestic and proprietary convictions in the breasts of vast majorities of their fellow-countrymen! And we incur this appalling risk for the want of a single, or at the most, a handful of Censors, invested with a simple but limitless discretion to excise or to suppress entirely such political utterances as may seem to their private judgments calculated to cause pain or moral disturbance in the average man. The masses, it is true, have their protection and remedy against injudicious or inflammatory politicians in the Law and the so-called democratic process of election; but we have seen that theatre audiences have also the protection of the Law, and the remedy of boycott, and that in their case, this protection and this remedy are not deemed enough. What, then, shall we say of the case of Politics, where the dangers attending inflammatory or subversive utterance are greater a million fold, and the remedy a thousand times less expeditious?

Our Legislators have laid down Censorship as the basic principle of Justice underlying the civic rights of dramatists. Then, let "Censorship for all" be their motto, and this country no longer be ridden and destroyed by free Institutions! Let them not only establish forthwith Censorships of Literature, Art, Science, and Religion, but also place themselves beneath the regimen with which they have calmly fettered Dramatic Authors. They cannot deem it becoming to their regard for justice, to their honour; to their sense of humour, to recoil from a restriction which, in a parallel case they have imposed on others. It is an old and homely saying that good officers never place their men in positions they would not themselves be willing to fill. And we are not entitled to believe that our Legislators, having set Dramatic Authors where they have been set, will—now that their duty is made plain—for a moment hesitate to step down and stand alongside.

But if by any chance they should recoil, and thus make answer: "We are ready at all times to submit to the Law and the People's will, and to bow to their demands, but we cannot and must not be asked to place our calling, our duty, and our honour beneath the irresponsible rule of an arbitrary autocrat, however sympathetic with the generality he may chance to be! " Then, we would ask: "Sirs, did you ever hear of that great saying: 'Do unto others as ye would they should do unto you! '" For it is but fair presumption that the Dramatists, whom our Legislators have placed in bondage to a despot, are, no less than those Legislators, proud of their calling, conscious of their duty, and jealous of their honour. 1909.

VAGUE THOUGHTS ON ART

It was on a day of rare beauty that I went out into the fields to try and gather these few thoughts. So golden and sweetly hot it was, that they came lazily, and with a flight no more coherent or responsible than the swoop of the very swallows; and, as in a play or poem, the result is conditioned by the conceiving mood, so I knew would be the nature of my diving, dipping, pale-throated, fork-tailed words. But, after all—I thought, sitting there—I need not take my critical pronouncements seriously. I have not the firm soul of the critic. It is not my profession to know 'things for certain, and to make others feel that certainty. On the contrary, I am often wrong—a luxury no critic can afford. And so, invading as I was the realm of others, I advanced with a light pen, feeling that none, and least of all myself, need expect me to be right.

What then—I thought—is Art? For I perceived that to think about it I must first define it; and I almost stopped thinking at all before the fearsome nature of that task. Then slowly in my mind gathered this group of words:

Art is that imaginative expression of human energy, which, through technical concretion of feeling and perception, tends to reconcile the individual with the universal, by exciting in him impersonal emotion. And the greatest Art is that which excites the greatest impersonal emotion in an hypothecated perfect human being.

Impersonal emotion! And what—I thought do I mean by that? Surely I mean: That is not Art, which, while I, am contemplating it, inspires me with any active or directive impulse; that is Art, when, for however brief a moment, it replaces within me interest in myself by interest in itself. For, let me suppose myself in the presence of a carved marble bath. If my thoughts be "What could I buy that for? " Impulse of acquisition; or: "From what quarry did it come? " Impulse of inquiry; or: "Which would be the right end for my head? " Mixed impulse of inquiry and acquisition—I am at that moment insensible to it as a work of Art. But, if I stand before it vibrating at sight of its colour and forms, if ever so little and for ever so short a time, unhaunted by any definite practical thought or impulse—to that extent and for that moment it has stolen me away out of myself and put itself there instead; has linked me to the universal by making me forget the individual in me. And for that moment, and only while that moment lasts, it is to me a work of Art. The word "impersonal, " then, is but used in this my definition to signify momentary forgetfulness of one's own personality and its active wants.

So Art—I thought—is that which, heard, read, or looked on, while producing no directive impulse, warms one with unconscious vibration. Nor can I imagine any means of defining what is the greatest Art, without hypothecating a perfect human being. But since we shall never see, or know if we do see, that desirable creature— dogmatism is banished, "Academy" is dead to the discussion, deader than even Tolstoy left it after his famous treatise "What is Art? " For, having destroyed all the old Judges and Academies, Tolstoy, by saying that the greatest Art was that which appealed to the greatest number of living human beings, raised up the masses of mankind to be a definite new Judge or Academy, as tyrannical and narrow as ever were those whom he had destroyed.

This, at all events—I thought is as far as I dare go in defining what Art is. But let me try to make plain to myself what is the essential quality that gives to Art the power of exciting this unconscious vibration, this impersonal emotion. It has been called Beauty! An awkward word—a perpetual begging of the question; too current in use, too ambiguous altogether; now too narrow, now too wide—a word, in fact, too glib to know at all what it means. And how dangerous a word—often misleading us into slabbing with extraneous floridities what would otherwise, on its own plane, be Art! To be decorative where decoration is not suitable, to be lyrical where lyricism is out of place, is assuredly to spoil Art, not to achieve it. But this essential quality of Art has also, and more happily, been called Rhythm. And, what is Rhythm if not that mysterious harmony between part and part, and part and whole, which gives what is called life; that exact proportion, the mystery of which is best grasped in observing how life leaves an animate creature when the essential relation of part to whole has been sufficiently disturbed. And I agree that this rhythmic relation of part to part, and part to whole—in short, vitality—is the one quality inseparable from a work of Art. For nothing which does not seem to a man possessed of this rhythmic vitality, can ever steal him out of himself.

And having got thus far in my thoughts, I paused, watching the swallows; for they seemed to me the symbol, in their swift, sure curvetting, all daring and balance and surprise, of the delicate poise and motion of Art, that visits no two men alike, in a world where no two things of all the things there be, are quite the same.

Yes—I thought—and this Art is the one form of human energy in the whole world, which really works for union, and destroys the barriers between man and man. It is the continual, unconscious replacement, however fleeting, of oneself by another; the real cement of human life; the everlasting refreshment and renewal. For, what is grievous, dompting, grim, about our lives is that we are shut up within ourselves, with an itch to get outside ourselves. And to be stolen away from ourselves by Art is a momentary relaxation from that itching, a minute's profound, and as it were secret, enfranchisement. The active amusements and relaxations of life can only rest certain of our faculties, by indulging others; the whole self is never rested save through that unconsciousness of self, which comes through rapt contemplation of Nature or of Art.

And suddenly I remembered that some believe that Art does not produce unconsciousness of self, but rather very vivid self-realisation.

Ah! but—I though—that is not the first and instant effect of Art; the new impetus is the after effect of that momentary replacement of oneself by the self of the work before us; it is surely the result of that brief span of enlargement, enfranchisement, and rest.

Yes, Art is the great and universal refreshment. For Art is never dogmatic; holds no brief for itself you may take it or you may leave it. It does not force itself rudely where it is not wanted. It is reverent to all tempers, to all points of view. But it is wilful—the very wind in the comings and goings of its influence, an uncapturable fugitive, visiting our hearts at vagrant, sweet moments; since we often stand even before the greatest works of Art without being able quite to lose ourselves! That restful oblivion comes, we never quite know when—and it is gone! But when it comes, it is a spirit hovering with cool wings, blessing us from least to greatest, according to our powers; a spirit deathless and varied as human life itself.

And in what sort of age—I thought—are artists living now? Are conditions favourable? Life is very multiple; full of "movements, " "facts, " and "news"; with the limelight terribly turned on—and all this is adverse to the artist. Yet, leisure is abundant; the facilities for study great; Liberty is respected—more or less. But, there is one great reason why, in this age of ours, Art, it seems, must flourish. For, just as cross-breeding in Nature—if it be not too violent—often gives an extra vitality to the offspring, so does cross-breeding of philosophies make for vitality in Art. I cannot help thinking that historians, looking back from the far future, will record this age as the Third

Renaissance. We who are lost in it, working or looking on, can neither tell what we are doing, nor where standing; but we cannot help observing, that, just as in the Greek Renaissance, worn-out Pagan orthodoxy was penetrated by new philosophy; just as in the Italian Renaissance, Pagan philosophy, reasserting itself, fertilised again an already too inbred Christian creed; so now Orthodoxy fertilised by Science is producing a fresh and fuller conception of life—a, love of Perfection, not for hope of reward, not for fear of punishment, but for Perfection's sake. Slowly, under our feet, beneath our consciousness, is forming that new philosophy, and it is in times of new philosophies that Art, itself in essence always a discovery, must flourish. Those whose sacred suns and moons are ever in the past, tell us that our Art is going to the dogs; and it is, indeed, true that we are in confusion! The waters are broken, and every nerve and sinew of the artist is strained to discover his own safety. It is an age of stir and change, a season of new wine and old bottles. Yet, assuredly, in spite of breakages and waste, a wine worth the drinking is all the time being made.

I ceased again to think, for the sun had dipped low, and the midges were biting me; and the sounds of evening had begun, those innumerable far-travelling sounds of man and bird and beast—so clear and intimate—of remote countrysides at sunset. And for long I listened, too vague to move my pen.

New philosophy—a vigorous Art! Are there not all the signs of it? In music, sculpture, painting; in fiction—and drama; in dancing; in criticism itself, if criticism be an Art. Yes, we are reaching out to a new faith not yet crystallised, to a new Art not yet perfected; the forms still to find-the flowers still to fashion!

And how has it come, this slowly growing faith in Perfection for Perfection's sake? Surely like this: The Western world awoke one day to find that it no longer believed corporately and for certain in future life for the individual consciousness. It began to feel: I cannot say more than that there may be—Death may be the end of man, or Death may be nothing. And it began to ask itself in this uncertainty: Do I then desire to go on living? Now, since it found that it desired to go on living at least as earnestly as ever it did before, it began to inquire why. And slowly it perceived that there was, inborn within it, a passionate instinct of which it had hardly till then been conscious—a sacred instinct to perfect itself, now, as well as in a possible hereafter; to perfect itself because Perfection was desirable, a vision to be adored, and striven for; a dream motive fastened within the Universe; the very essential Cause of everything. And it began to see that this Perfection, cosmically, was nothing but perfect Equanimity and Harmony; and in human relations, nothing but perfect Love and Justice. And Perfection began to glow before the eyes of the Western world like a new star, whose light touched with glamour all things as they came forth from Mystery, till to Mystery they were ready to return.

This—I thought is surely what the Western world has dimly been rediscovering. There has crept into our minds once more the feeling that the Universe is all of a piece, Equipoise supreme; and all things equally wonderful, and mysterious, and valuable. We have begun, in fact, to have a glimmering of the artist's creed, that nothing may we despise or neglect—that everything is worth the doing well, the making fair—that our God, Perfection, is implicit everywhere, and the revelation of Him the business of our Art.

And as I jotted down these words I noticed that some real stars had crept up into the sky, so gradually darkening above the pollard lime-trees; cuckoos, who had been calling on the thorn-trees all the afternoon, were silent; the swallows no longer flirted past, but a bat was already in career over the holly hedge; and round me the buttercups were closing. The whole form and feeling of the world had changed, so that I seemed to have before me a new picture hanging.

Ah! I thought Art must indeed be priest of this new faith in Perfection, whose motto is: "Harmony, Proportion, Balance. " For by Art alone can true harmony in human affairs be fostered, true Proportion revealed, and true Equipoise preserved. Is not the training of an artist a training in the due relation of one thing with another, and in the faculty of expressing that relation clearly; and, even more, a training in the faculty of disengaging from self the very essence of self—and passing that essence into other selves by so delicate means that none shall see how it is done, yet be insensibly unified? Is not the artist, of all men, foe and nullifier of partisanship and parochialism, of distortions and extravagance, the discoverer of that jack-o'-lantern—Truth; for, if Truth be not Spiritual Proportion I know not what it is. Truth it seems to me—is no absolute thing, but always relative, the essential symmetry in the varying relationships of life; and the most perfect truth is but the concrete expression of the most penetrating vision. Life seen throughout as a countless show of the finest works of Art; Life shaped, and purged of the irrelevant, the gross, and the extravagant; Life, as it were, spiritually selected—that is Truth; a thing as multiple, and changing, as subtle, and strange, as Life itself, and as little to be bound by dogma. Truth admits but the one rule: No deficiency, and no excess! Disobedient to that rule—nothing attains full vitality. And secretly fettered by that rule is Art, whose business is the creation of vital things.

That aesthete, to be sure, was right, when he said: "It is Style that makes one believe in a thing; nothing but Style. " For, what is Style in its true and broadest sense save fidelity to idea and mood, and perfect balance in the clothing of them? And I thought: Can one believe in the decadence of Art in an age which, however unconsciously as yet, is beginning to worship that which Art worships—Perfection-Style?

The faults of our Arts to-day are the faults of zeal and of adventure, the faults and crudities of pioneers, the errors and mishaps of the explorer. They must pass through many fevers, and many times lose their way; but at all events they shall not go dying in their beds, and be buried at Kensal Green. And, here and there, amid the disasters and wreckage of their voyages of discovery, they will find something new, some fresh way of embellishing life, or of revealing the heart of things. That characteristic of to-day's Art—the striving of each branch of Art to burst its own boundaries—which to many spells destruction, is surely of happy omen. The novel straining to become the play, the play the novel, both trying to paint; music striving to become story; poetry gasping to be music; painting panting to be philosophy; forms, canons, rules, all melting in the pot; stagnation broken up! In all this havoc there is much to shock and jar even the most eager and adventurous. We cannot stand these new-fangled fellows! They have no form! They rush in where angels fear to tread. They have lost all the good of the old, and given us nothing in its place! And yet—only out of stir and change is born new salvation. To deny that is to deny belief in man, to turn our backs on courage! It is well, indeed, that some should live in closed studies with the paintings and the books of yesterday—such devoted students serve Art in their own way. But the fresh-air world will ever want new forms. We shall not get them without faith enough to risk the old! The good will live, the bad will die; and tomorrow only can tell us which is which!

Yes—I thought—we naturally take a too impatient view of the Art of our own time, since we can neither see the ends toward which it is almost blindly groping, nor the few perfected creations that will be left standing amidst the rubble of abortive effort. An age must always decry itself and extol its forbears. The unwritten history of every Art will show us that. Consider the novel—that most recent form of Art! Did not the age which followed Fielding lament the treachery of authors to the Picaresque tradition, complaining that they were not as Fielding and Smollett were? Be sure they did. Very slowly and in spite of opposition did the novel attain in this country the fulness of that biographical form achieved under Thackeray. Very slowly, and in face of condemnation, it has been losing that form in favour of a greater vividness which places before the reader's brain, not historical statements, as it were, of motives and of facts, but word-paintings of things and persons, so chosen and arranged that the reader may see, as if at first hand, the spirit of Life at work before him. The new novel has as many bemoaners as the old novel had when it was new. It is no question of better or worse, but of differing forms—of change dictated by gradual suitability to the changing conditions of our social life, and to the ever fresh discoveries of craftsmen, in the intoxication of which, old and equally worthy craftsmanship is—by the way—too often for the moment mislaid. The vested interests of life favour the line of least resistance—disliking and revolting against disturbance; but one must always remember that a spurious glamour is inclined to gather around what is new. And, because of these two deflecting factors, those who break through old forms must well expect to be dead before the new forms they have unconsciously created have found their true level, high or low, in the world of Art. When a thing is new how shall it be judged? In the fluster of meeting novelty, we have even seen coherence attempting to bind together two personalities so fundamentally opposed as those of Ibsen and Bernard Shaw dramatists with hardly a quality in common; no identity of tradition, or belief; not the faintest resemblance in methods of construction or technique. Yet contemporary; estimate talks of them often in the same breath. They are new! It is enough. And others, as utterly unlike them both. They too are new. They have as yet no label of their own then put on some one else's!

And so—I thought it must always be; for Time is essential to the proper placing and estimate of all Art. And is it not this feeling, that contemporary judgments are apt to turn out a little ludicrous, which has converted much criticism of late from judgment pronounced into impression recorded—recreative statement—a kind, in fact, of expression of the critic's self, elicited through contemplation of a book, a play, a symphony, a picture? For this kind of criticism there has even recently been claimed an actual identity with creation. Esthetic judgment and creative power identical! That is a hard saying. For, however sympathetic one may feel toward this new criticism, however one may recognise that the recording of impression has a wider, more elastic, and more lasting value than the delivery of arbitrary judgment based on rigid laws of taste; however one may admit that it approaches the creative gift in so far as it demands the qualities of receptivity and reproduction— is there not still lacking to this "new" critic something of that thirsting spirit of discovery, which precedes the creation—hitherto so-called—of anything? Criticism, taste, aesthetic judgment, by the very nature of their task, wait till life has been focussed by the artists before they attempt to reproduce the image which that imprisoned fragment of life makes on the mirror of their minds. But a thing created springs from a germ unconsciously implanted by the direct impact of unfettered life on the whole range, of the creator's temperament; and round the germ thus engendered, the creative artist—ever penetrating, discovering, selecting—goes on building cell on cell, gathered from a million little fresh impacts and visions. And to say that this is also exactly what the recreative critic does, is to say that the interpretative musician is creator in the same sense as is the composer of the music that he interprets. If, indeed, these processes be the same in kind, they are in degree so far apart that one would think the word creative unfortunately used of both....

But this speculation—I thought—is going beyond the bounds of vagueness. Let there be some thread of coherence in your thoughts, as there is in the progress of this evening, fast fading into night. Return to the consideration of the nature and purposes of Art! And recognize that much of what you have thought will seem on the face of it heresy to the school whose doctrine was incarnated by Oscar Wilde in that admirable apotheosis of half-truths: "The Decay of the Art of Lying. " For therein he said: "No great artist ever sees things as they really are. " Yet, that half-truth might also be put thus: The seeing of things as they really are—the seeing of a proportion veiled from other eyes (together with the power of expression), is what makes a man an artist. What makes him a great artist is a high fervour of spirit, which produces a superlative, instead of a comparative, clarity of vision.

Close to my house there is a group of pines with gnarled red limbs flanked by beech-trees. And there is often a very deep blue sky behind. Generally, that is all I see. But, once in a way, in those trees against that sky I seem to see all the passionate life and glow that Titian painted into his pagan pictures. I have a vision of mysterious meaning, of a mysterious relation between that sky and those trees with their gnarled red limbs and Life as I know it. And when I have had that vision I always feel, this is reality, and all those other times, when I have no such vision, simple unreality. If I were a painter, it is for such fervent vision I should wait, before moving brush: This, so intimate, inner vision of reality, indeed, seems in duller moments well-nigh grotesque; and hence that other glib half-truth: "Art is greater than Life itself. " Art is, indeed, greater than Life in the sense that the power of Art is the disengagement from Life of its real spirit and significance. But in any other sense, to say that Art is greater than Life from which it emerges, and into which it must remerge, can but suspend the artist over Life, with his feet in the air and his head in the clouds—Prig masquerading as Demi-god. "Nature is no great Mother who has borne us. She is our creation. It is in our brain that she quickens to life. " Such is the highest hyperbole of the aesthetic creed. But what is creative instinct, if not an incessant living sympathy with Nature, a constant craving like that of Nature's own, to fashion something new out of all that comes within the grasp of those faculties with which Nature has endowed us? The qualities of vision, of fancy, and of imaginative power, are no more divorced from Nature, than are the qualities of common-sense and courage. They are rarer, that is all.

But in truth, no one holds such views. Not even those who utter them. They are the rhetoric, the over-statement of half-truths, by such as wish to condemn what they call "Realism, " without being temperamentally capable of understanding what "Realism" really is.

And what—I thought—is Realism? What is the meaning of that word so wildly used? Is it descriptive of technique, or descriptive of the spirit of the artist; or both, or neither? Was Turgenev a realist? No greater poet ever wrote in prose, nor any one who more closely brought the actual shapes of men and things before us. No more fervent idealists than Ibsen and Tolstoy ever lived; and none more careful to make their people real. Were they realists? No more deeply fantastic writer can I conceive than Dostoievsky, nor any who has described actual situations more vividly. Was he a realist? The late Stephen Crane was called a realist. Than whom no more impressionistic writer ever painted with words. What then is the heart of this term still often used as an expression almost of abuse? To me, at all events—I thought—the words realism, realistic, have no longer reference to technique, for which the words naturalism, naturalistic, serve far better. Nor have they to do with the question of imaginative power—as much demanded by realism as by romanticism. For me, a realist is by no means tied to naturalistic technique—he may be poetic, idealistic, fantastic, impressionistic, anything but— romantic; that, in so far as he is a realist, he cannot be. The word, in fact, characterises that artist whose temperamental preoccupation is with revelation of the actual inter-relating spirit of life, character, and thought, with a view to enlighten himself and others; as distinguished from that artist whom I call romantic—whose tempera mental purpose is invention of tale or design with a view to delight himself and others. It is a question of temperamental antecedent motive in the artist, and nothing more.

Realist—Romanticist! Enlightenment—Delight! That is the true apposition. To make a revelation—to tell a fairy-tale! And either of these artists may use what form he likes—naturalistic, fantastic, poetic, impressionistic. For it is not by the form, but by the purpose and mood of his art that he shall be known, as one or as the other. Realists indeed—including the half of Shakespeare that was realist not being primarily concerned to amuse their audience, are still comparatively unpopular in a world made up for the greater part of men of action, who instinctively reject all art that does not distract them without causing them to think. For thought makes demands on an energy already in full use; thought causes introspection; and introspection causes discomfort, and disturbs the grooves of action. To say that the object of the realist is to enlighten rather than to delight, is not to say that in his art the realist is not amusing himself as much as ever is the teller of a fairy-tale, though he does not deliberately start out to do so; he is amusing, too, a large part of mankind. For, admitted that the abject, and the test of Art, is always the awakening of vibration, of impersonal emotion, it is still usually forgotten that men fall, roughly speaking, into two flocks: Those whose intelligence is uninquiring in the face of Art, and does not demand to be appeased before their emotions can be stirred; and those who, having a speculative bent of mind, must first be satisfied by an enlightening quality in a work of Art, before that work of Art can awaken in them feeling. The audience of the realist is drawn from this latter type of man; the much larger audience of the romantic artist from the former; together with, in both cases, those fastidious few for whom all Art is style and only style, and who welcome either kind, so long as it is good enough.

To me, then—I thought—this division into Realism and Romance, so understood, is the main cleavage in all the Arts; but it is hard to find pure examples of either kind. For even the most determined realist has more than a streak in him of the romanticist, and the most resolute romanticist finds it impossible at times to be quite unreal. Guido Reni, Watteau, Leighton were they not perhaps somewhat pure romanticists; Rembrandt, Hogarth, Manet mainly realists; Botticelli, Titian, Raphael, a blend. Dumas pere, and Scott, surely romantic; Flaubert and Tolstoy as surely realists; Dickens and Cervantes, blended. Keats and Swinburne romantic; Browning and Whitman—realistic; Shakespeare and Goethe, both. The Greek dramatists—realists. The Arabian Nights and Malory romantic. The Iliad, the Odyssey, and the Old Testament, both realism and romance. And if in the vagueness of my thoughts I were to seek for illustration less general and vague to show the essence of this temperamental cleavage in all Art, I would take the two novelists Turgenev and Stevenson. For Turgenev expressed himself in stories that must be called romances, and Stevenson employed almost always a naturalistic technique. Yet no one would ever call Turgenev a romanticist, or Stevenson a realist. The spirit of the first brooded over life, found in it a perpetual voyage of spiritual adventure, was set on discovering and making clear to himself and all, the varying traits and emotions of human character—the varying moods of Nature; and though he couched all this discovery in caskets of engaging story, it was always clear as day what mood it was that drove him to dip pen in ink. The spirit of the second, I think, almost dreaded to discover; he felt life, I believe, too keenly to want to probe into it; he spun his gossamer to lure himself and all away from life. That was his driving mood; but the craftsman in him, longing to be clear and poignant, made him more natural, more actual than most realists.

So, how thin often is the hedge! And how poor a business the partisan abuse of either kind of art in a world where each sort of mind has full right to its own due expression, and grumbling lawful only when due expression is not attained. One may not care for a Rembrandt portrait of a plain old woman; a graceful Watteau decoration may leave another cold but foolish will he be who denies that both are faithful to their conceiving moods, and so proportioned part to part, and part to whole, as to have, each in its own way, that inherent rhythm or vitality which is the hall-mark of Art. He is but a poor philosopher who holds a view so narrow as to exclude forms not to his personal taste. No realist can love romantic Art so much as he loves his own, but when that Art fulfils the laws of its peculiar being, if he would be no blind partisan, he must admit it. The romanticist will never be amused by realism, but let him not for that reason be so parochial as to think that realism, when it achieves vitality, is not Art. For what is Art but the perfected expression of self in contact with the world; and whether that self be of enlightening, or of fairy-telling temperament, is of no moment whatsoever. The tossing of abuse from realist to romanticist and back is but the sword-play of two one-eyed men with their blind side turned toward each other. Shall not each attempt be judged on its own merits? If found not shoddy, faked, or forced, but true to itself, true to its conceiving mood, and fair-proportioned part to whole; so that it lives—then, realistic or romantic, in the name of Fairness let it pass! Of all kinds of human energy, Art is surely the most free, the least parochial; and demands of us an essential tolerance of all its forms. Shall we waste breath and ink in condemnation of artists, because their temperaments are not our own?

But the shapes and colours of the day were now all blurred; every tree and stone entangled in the dusk. How different the world seemed from that in which I had first sat down, with the swallows flirting past. And my mood was different; for each of those worlds had brought to my heart its proper feeling—painted on my eyes the just picture. And Night, that was coming, would bring me yet another mood that would frame itself with consciousness at its own fair moment, and hang before me. A quiet owl stole by in the geld below, and vanished into the heart of a tree. And suddenly above the moor-line I saw the large moon rising. Cinnamon-coloured, it made all things swim, made me uncertain of my thoughts, vague with mazy feeling. Shapes seemed but drifts of moon-dust, and true reality nothing save a sort of still listening to the wind. And for long I sat, just watching the moon creep up, and hearing the thin, dry rustle of the leaves along the holly hedge. And there came to me this thought: What is this Universe—that never had beginning and will never have an end—but a myriad striving to perfect pictures never the same, so blending and fading one into another, that all form one great perfected picture? And what are we—ripples on the tides of a birthless, deathless, equipoised Creative-Purpose—but little works of Art?

Trying to record that thought, I noticed that my note-book was damp with dew. The cattle were lying down. It was too dark to see. 1911

BiB Id : 35100
068516
814
19/1/10
SR

Lightning Source UK Ltd.
Milton Keynes UK
03 December 2009

147017UK00002B/136/P